10-FOLD
ORIGAMI

10-FOLD
ORIGAMI

Fabulous Paperfolds You Can Make in Just 10 Steps!

PETER ENGEL

TUTTLE PUBLISHING
Tokyo • Rutland, Vermont • Singapore

To Cheryl, Hannah, and Gabriel,
forever folded in each other's universe

Published by Tuttle Publishing, an imprint of Periplus Editions (HK) Ltd.

www.tuttlepublishing.com

Library of Congress Control Number: 2009920075

ISBN 978-4-8053-1069-4

Distributed by

North America, Latin America & Europe
Tuttle Publishing
364 Innovation Drive
North Clarendon
VT 05759-9436 U.S.A.
Tel: 1 (802) 773-8930
Fax: 1 (802) 773-6993
info@tuttlepublishing.com
www.tuttlepublishing.com

Japan
Tuttle Publishing
Yaekari Building, 3rd Floor
5-4-12 Osaki, Shinagawa-ku
Tokyo 141 0032
Tel: (81) 3 5437-0171
Fax: (81) 3 5437-0755
tuttle-sales@gol.com

Asia Pacific
Berkeley Books Pte. Ltd.
61 Tai Seng Avenue #02-12,
Singapore 534167
Tel: (65) 6280-1330
Fax: (65) 6280-6290
inquiries@periplus.com.sg
www.periplus.com

First edition
14 13 12 11 10   10 9 8 7 6 5 4 3

Printed in Singapore

Photography by Allan Penn
Cover and interior design by 3+Co.

TUTTLE PUBLISHING® is a registered trademark of Tuttle Publishing, a division of Periplus Editions (HK) Ltd.

CONTENTS

Easy: ✳			
Intermediate: ✦	✳	✦	❖
Advanced: ❖	Easy	Int.	Adv.

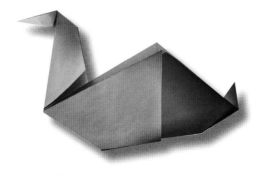

INTRODUCTION

Origami is a playful art and an artful form of play

Around the world, children who delight in the paper cup, the fortune teller, the jumping frog, and the water bomb (a paper cube that you inflate and fill with water to toss at enemies) little suspect that this ancient entertainment is an artform deeply connected to haiku, Japanese brush painting, Zen garden design, and even modern sculpture and architecture. In common with these genres, origami is a minimalist art. The success of a completed origami design is determined by its ability to express the most with the least. Called a "model" by paperfolders, a finished project should capture the essence of its subject matter by means of abstraction, form, proportion, movement, symmetry, and asymmetry, as well as an intangible quality that speaks to the heart and soul.

Paperfolders familiar with my work will know that many of my designs are extremely complex, often involving fifty steps or more. Inventing the much sim-

pler models for this book has been both a pleasure and a challenge, proving to me that as a minimalist I have a long way to go. Each of these models can be folded in ten steps (or fewer), but within a single step there may be a sequence of folds that are closely related. The process of folding is, in fact, a continuum of movement, broken down into illustrated steps the way that a motion picture divides continuous action into discrete frames. Although limited to ten numbered steps, these models vary greatly in complexity. Beginning folders are encouraged to tackle the easier ones first in order to build skill and confidence. Even veteran folders may find that it takes more than one attempt at a complicated design to produce a satisfying result. For those who persevere, I can guarantee that this will be the most enjoyable ten-step program you ever undertake.

The models in this book can all be made from commercially available origami paper, such as the approximately 6- and 10-inch (15- and 25-cm) squares found at arts and crafts stores. To fold a model of a given size, calculate the size of the initial square from the information given on the first page of each set of diagrams. Although origami paper is comparatively inexpensive, I encourage readers to experiment with art paper of higher quality. Handmade Japanese washi paper is durable and comes in myriad textures, styles, patterns, and colors. If the paper is molded when it is damp (misting it with a plant sprayer), it will retain its shape when dry. Useful tools include tweezers with an elongated tip and a burnisher, which is any tool with a flat edge or tip (hardware stores often stock metal ones that resemble a dentist's tools).

Before you start, here are a few notes on the

models. The book starts with **Traditionals**, simple and enduring designs intended to flex the fingers of beginning folders. The last of the models in this chapter, the *Sailboat*, is the symbol of Origami USA and was a favorite of that organization's founder, Lillian Oppenheimer. The remainder of the models in the book (with one exception) are my own design. **Delectables** begins with a tribute to the friendly service and dreadful cuisine of the diners that I frequented while growing up in New York City. Starting with the idea of a fried egg, my first design for *Sunny Side Up* proved pleasing (it has an inflatable yolk) but seemed beyond the reach of a short-order paperfolder (too many steps), so I have replaced it here with a simpler version. The *Plate* is the first published design by Gabriel Perko-Engel, a promising young folder to keep an eye on.

At the heart of **For the Romantic** are a *High-Heeled Shoe* and a *Wedding Ring* designed at the urging of my stylish editor, Wendy Gardner. The *Butterfly* was inspired by the mesmerizing display of Monarch butterflies that migrate up and down the California coast, washing the sky and trees a brilliant orange. **Wild Kingdom** includes my second design of an asymmetric snake (which is far simpler than my original version that coils) as well as simplified versions of my *Penguin* and *Bat*. Less exotic but still fascinating, the *Snail on a Leaf* pays homage to the inhabitants of my overgrown yard. **Just for Fun** features a *Rocket Ship* that I invented as a child and a *Spinner* and *Hatching Chick* invented about three and a half decades later, proving that you never can take the paperfolder out of the man. With its focus on playful art and artful play, **Just for Fun** brings the book to a fitting close. Enjoy!

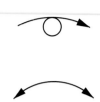

BASIC ORIGAMI SYMBOLS AND FOLDS

Origami diagrams are like a composer's score or an architect's plans: They are the key to interpreting the design and the means by which the performer or builder realizes the creator's intentions. Learning to read folding instructions takes practice, just like learning to follow a musical score. The basic folding procedures and symbols used in these diagrams follow an internationally accepted standard. When you have mastered the ones here, you should be able to follow the instructions in virtually any origami book.

A couple of arrows have specific meanings. The top arrow means "turn the paper over." The bottom arrow, with two heads, means "fold and unfold."

SYMBOLS

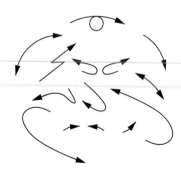

Symbols consist of two types: arrows and lines. There are many types of arrows, whose expressive shapes suggest the motion of the paper.

There are six types of lines used in this book:

- A thick line shows the outline of the diagram against the page.
- A *medium* line represents an edge of the paper, either the original edge or one produced by folding.
- A *thin* line represents a crease in the paper that was formed in an earlier step.
- A *dashed* line represents a valley-fold.
- A *dotted* and dashed line represents a mountain-fold.
- A *dotted* line represents a fold hidden from view or, occasionally, a fold about to be formed.

BASIC FOLDS

A piece of paper has two sides. Thus, it can be folded in either of two directions. Each of these folds has a name: valley-fold and mountain-fold. Every origami folding procedure is a valley-fold, a mountain-fold, or a combination of valley- and mountain-folds.

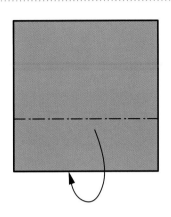

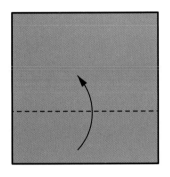

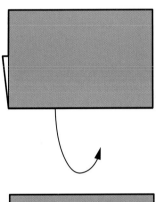

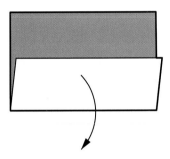

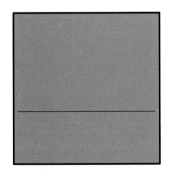

Forming a mountain-fold:

Swing the lower edge underneath to produce a mountain-fold. If you swing the lower edge back, a thin line indicates where the paper has been creased.

A *reverse-fold* combines valley-folds and mountain-folds. In a reverse-fold, two or more layers of paper are folded together symmetrically along a single crease. The reverse-fold comes in two types: *inside reverse-fold* (the more common) and *outside reverse-fold*.

Forming a valley-fold

Swing the lower edge upward to produce a valley-fold. If you swing the lower edge back down, a thin line indicates where the paper has been creased.

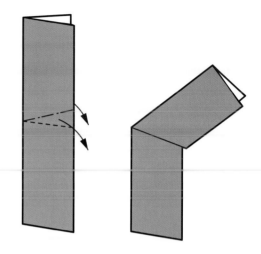

In a *crimp-fold*, a pair of valley-folds and mountain-folds converges at one point. The creases on the front and rear layers are mirror images of each other.

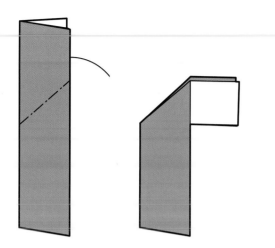

Forming an inside reverse-fold:

Crease firmly with either a mountain- or a valley-fold to form the line of the reverse-fold. Spread the open edges of the paper and turn the top portion inside-out by pushing inward on the crease of the mountain- or valley-fold. Flatten to form an inside reverse-fold.

Forming a crimp-fold:

Valley-fold and mountain-fold the front and back. Flatten to form a crimp-fold.

In a *pleat-fold*, a mountain- and a valley-fold are parallel. A pleat can be performed on any number of layers. They are folded together as one.

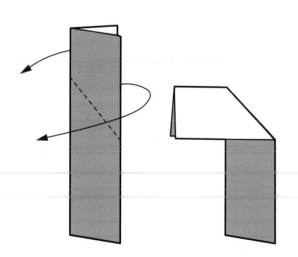

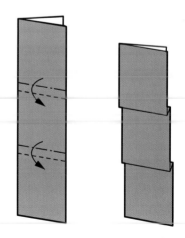

Forming an outside reverse-fold:

Crease firmly with either a mountain- or a valley-fold to form the line of the reverse-fold. Spread the open edges of the paper and turn the top portion outside-in. Flatten to form an outside reverse-fold.

Forming a pleat-fold:

Valley-fold and mountain-fold the front and back. Flatten to form a pleat-fold.

One other procedure merits special attention. A *sink-fold* is a kind of 3-D reverse-fold. In a sink-fold, a portion of the middle of the paper is reversed back into the paper (and may be reversed back out again, as desired).

Paying attention to a few folding tips will improve your results.

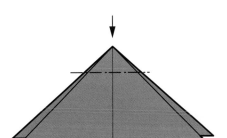

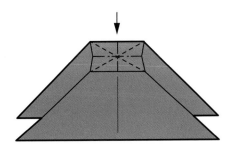

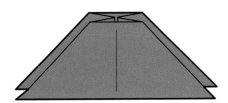

- Study each diagram carefully and read the accompanying text before commencing a fold. Look ahead to the next diagram to examine the result.

- Make creases crisp. A sloppy fold made early on will grow even sloppier over the course of folding.

- Remember that paper has a thickness. Layers of paper accumulate and may reach 1/8 inch (.3 cm) in more complicated models. It is often best to leave space between two adjacent edges so that they will not overlap and bunch in subsequent folds.

- Be patient. A careless maneuver in the late stage of a model can rip the paper and mar the result. If a model proves too complicated, try another, and then return to the first. The initial attempt at folding a model rarely yields a masterpiece, but repeated tries will eventually produce a model that you can be proud of.

Forming a sink-fold:
Crease firmly with either a mountain- or a valley-fold to form the line of the sink-fold. Spread the center of the paper and push the upper portion downward. The upper portion of the paper will flatten and then turn inside-out. Flatten to form the sink-fold.

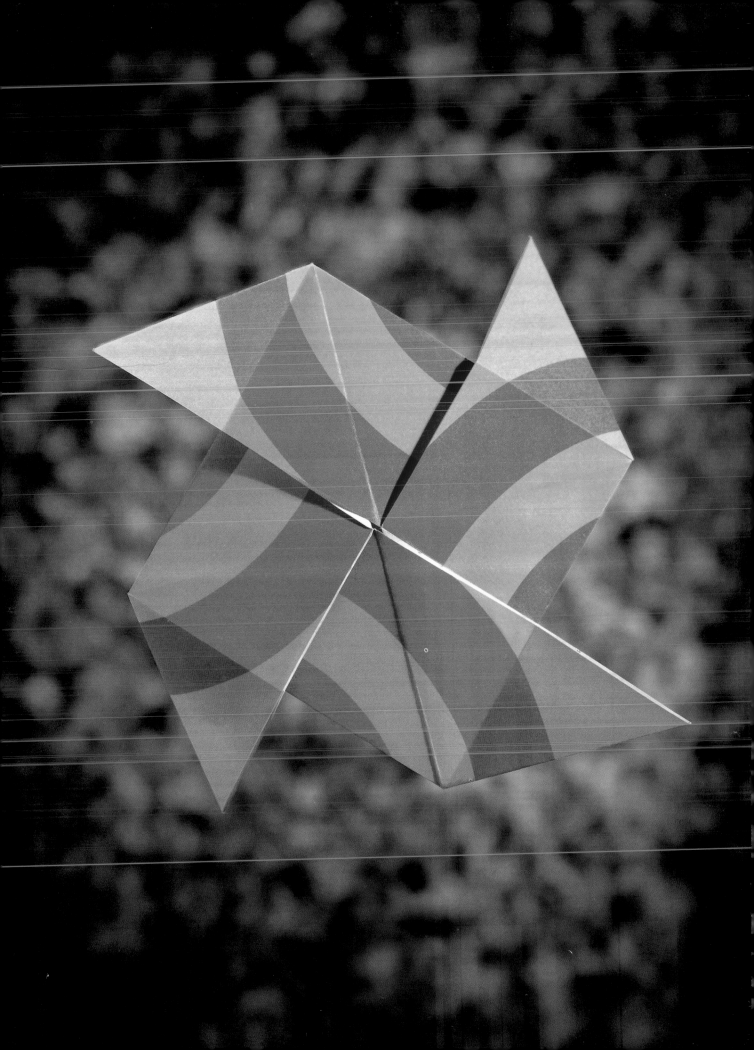

Chapter 1

TRADITIONALS

DUCK

A 10-inch (25-cm) square produces a duck that is 9 1/2 inches (24 cm) long from beak to tail.

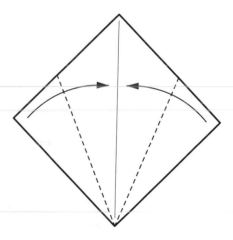

1. Precrease one diagonal. Valley-fold edges to centerline.

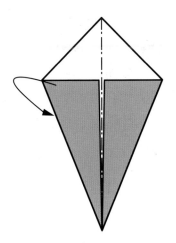

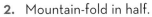

2. Mountain-fold in half.

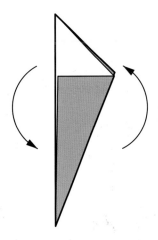

3. Rotate to horizontal.

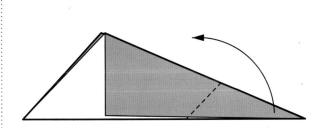

4. Valley-fold neck upward.

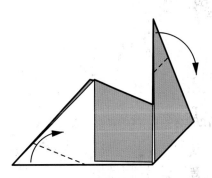

5. Valley-fold rear of body to form tail and neck to form head. As a variation, return the model to its position in step 4 and perform steps 4 and 5 with reverse-folds.

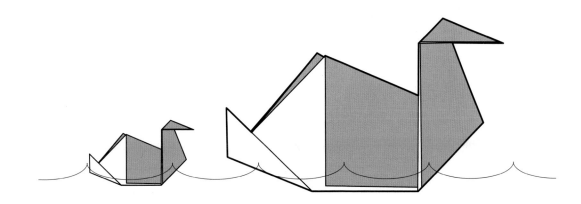

Completed Duck.

HOUSE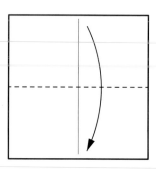

A 10-inch (25-cm) square produces a house
that is 5 inches (13 cm) tall.

1.   Precrease vertical centerline. Valley-fold in
     half.

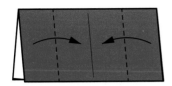

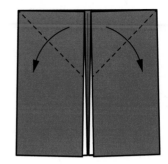

2. Valley-fold edges to centerline

3. Valley-fold corners down.

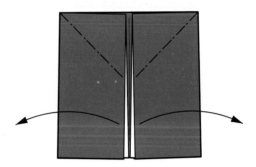

4. Swing corners back up.

5. Insert thumbs between top and middle layer of paper at the "foundation" of the house and separate these layers outward to expand the house, spreading the corners in the process. Flatten.

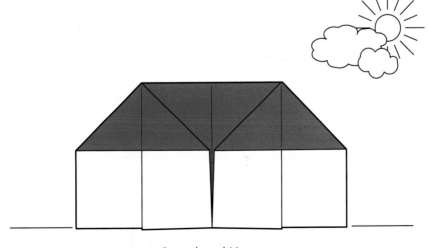

Completed House.

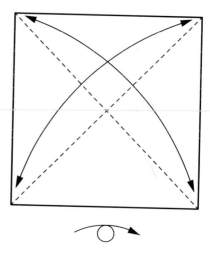

1. Valley-fold diagonals and unfold. Turn over.

PINWHEEL

A 10-inch (25-cm) square produces a pinwheel that is 10 inches (25 cm) from tip to opposite tip.

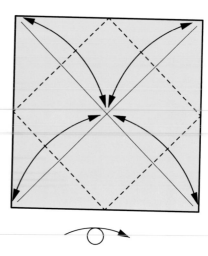

2. Valley-fold corners to center and unfold. Turn over.

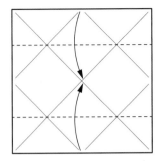

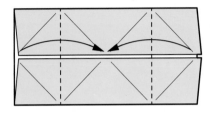

3. Valley-fold top and bottom edges to center.

4. Valley-fold side edges to center.

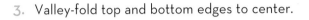

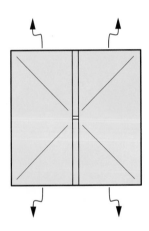

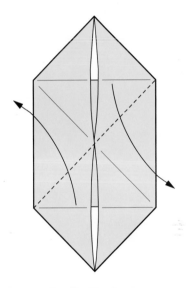

5. Pull out loose paper at top and bottom.

6. Swing the upper right corner down to the right and the lower left corner up to the left. Spread flaps slightly to catch the wind.

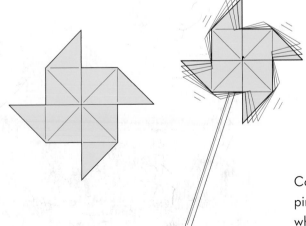

Completed Pinwheel. Pierce the center with a pin and insert the pin into a stick to allow the pinwheel to rotate in the breeze.

SAILBOAT ✳ Easy

A 10-inch (25-cm) square produces a sailboat that
is 7 inches (18 cm) from stem to stern.

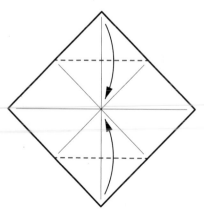

1. Precrease horizontals, verticals, and diagonals.
   Valley-fold top and bottom corners to center.

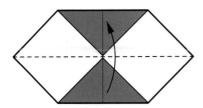

2. Valley-fold in half from bottom to top.

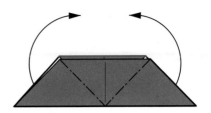

3. Reverse-fold corners to centerline.

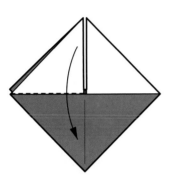

4. Valley-fold one sail down along colored edge.

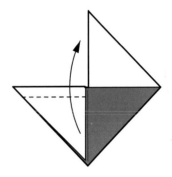

5. Valley-fold sail back up along a new crease.

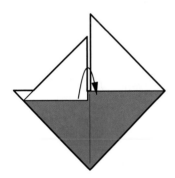

6. Tuck sail into hull.

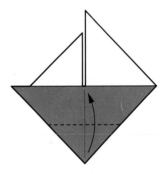

7. Valley-fold bottom point to centerline.

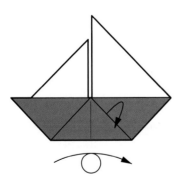

8. Release corner to form a stand. Turn over.

Completed Sailboat. Tilt back slightly and it will stand.

Chapter 2

....

DELECTABLES

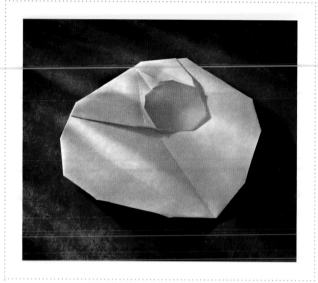

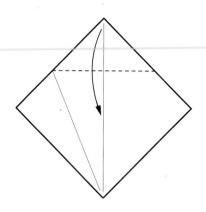

2. Lightly valley-fold top down. Unfold.

Breakfast Special

SUNNY
SIDE UP

A 7 ½-inch (19-cm) square produces an egg that is 5 inches (13 cm) in diameter. Follow the indicated dimensions for the bacon and plate to ensure that all three are proportional.

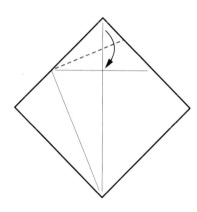

3. Lightly valley-fold upper left-hand edge to meet horizontal crease. Unfold.

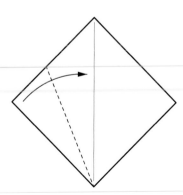

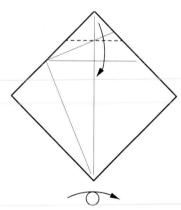

1. Precrease vertical centerline. Lightly valley-fold one edge to the centerline. Unfold.

4. Firmly valley-fold tip down where angled crease crosses centerline. Turn over.

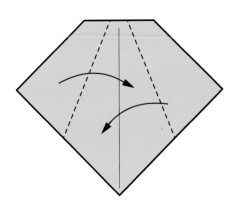

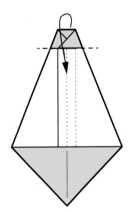

5. Valley-fold so that upper left-hand and right-hand edges cross the centerline and become vertical. There is no exact location for these folds, but make both sides the same.

6. Valley-fold colored tip down where it meets the white paper. Allow point to release from the back.

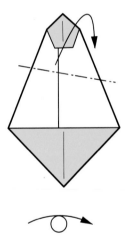

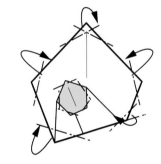

7. Mountain-fold upper portion over to the back and turn model over. See next diagram for approximate location of fold.

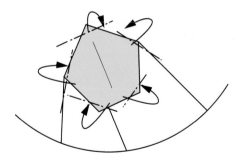

8. Round corners as desired with mountain-folds—see close-up for tiny folds at the yolk.

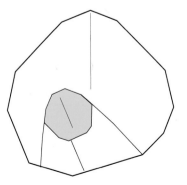

Completed Sunny Side Up.

BACON ✳ Easy

A 6 ¹/₂-inch (16- to 17-cm) square produces a strip of bacon that is 6 inches (15 cm) long.

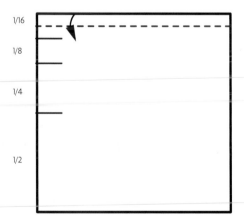

1. Lightly valley-fold paper in half repeatedly to produce a light line at the ¹/₁₆ point. Unfold.

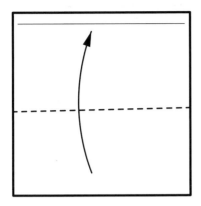

2. Valley-fold bottom edge to line at a slight angle.

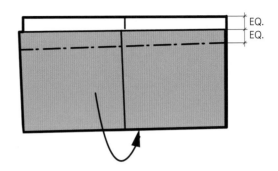

3. Mountain-fold at another slight angle.

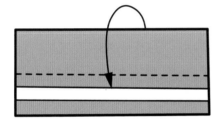

4. Valley-fold at another slight angle and tuck under white flap.

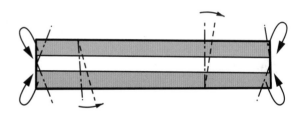

5. Mountain-fold corners. Crimp interior at two locations.

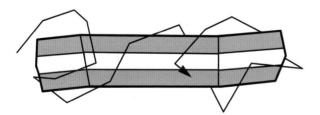

6. Crumple into a tiny ball and unfold.

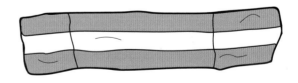

Completed Bacon.

PLATE

Int.

Designed by Gabriel Perko-Engel

An 11 3/4-inch (30-cm) square produces a plate that is 9 inches (23 cm) in diameter.

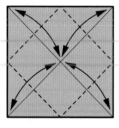

1. Precrease diagonals. Valley-fold corners to center and unfold.

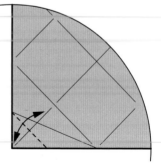

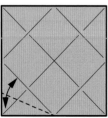

2. Valley-fold lower left edge to diagonal crease and unfold.

3. Enlargement of lower left-hand corner. Valley-fold where angled crease from step 2 meets edge. Unfold.

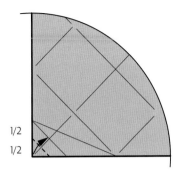

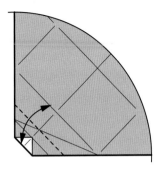

4. Valley-fold tip to crease produced in step 3.

5. Valley-fold where crease produced in step 2 meets main diagonal. White paper will not meet existing diagonal crease. Unfold.

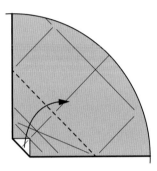

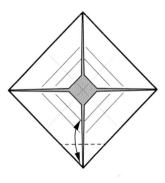

6. Valley-fold on existing diagonal crease. Repeat steps 2 through 6 on the other three corners.

7. Valley-fold lower point to where innermost pair of angled creases meet vertical edge. Unfold.

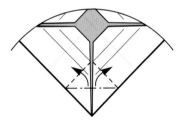

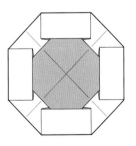

8. Lift and spread at horizontal crease formed in previous step, then flatten.

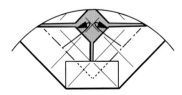

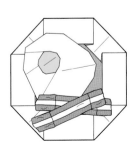

Complete Plate & Breakfast Special— as savory as the real thing, and without the calories.

9. Mountain-fold adjacent white flaps along outermost angled creases. Repeat steps 7 through 9 on the remaining three corners.

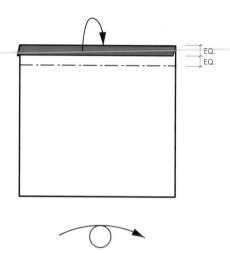

2. Mountain-fold top to produce two equal strips. Turn paper over.

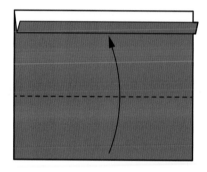

3. Valley-fold bottom edge up to meet colored edge.

CANDY CANE

Int.

A 10-inch (25-cm) square produces a candy cane that is 6 inches (15 cm) tall.

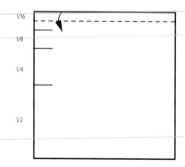

1. Lightly fold in half horizontally to produce lines at the $1/8$ and $1/16$ point. Valley-fold at the $1/16$ point.

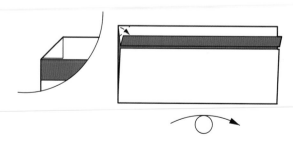

4. Valley-fold upper left-hand corner down, then unfold. Turn over.

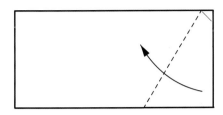

5. Valley-fold lower right-hand portion of paper up and to the left. See next step for exact location of fold.

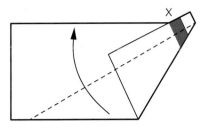

6. Point X, where two edges meet at the corner of colored portion, determines location of fold in previous step. Valley-fold lower right-hand portion of paper so that right-hand edge meets top edge.

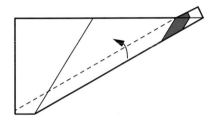

7. Roll lower right-hand strip over so that valley-fold meets red portion in upper right. New fold should be parallel to fold made in previous step. Lower left-hand part of valley-fold may not meet corner. Continue rolling paper until it resembles step 8.

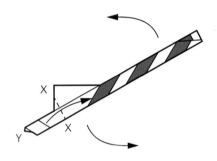

8. Valley-fold from X to X where hidden red flap comes to a point—see step 9 for reference. Tuck tip Y under the first red stripe. Rotate model.

9. Valley-fold twice at bottom to tuck flap Z into pocket behind.

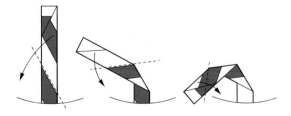

9A-9C.
Make three valley-folds at top of candy cane to form hook. If the hook will not lie flat, alternate valley- and mountain-folds.

Completed Candy Cane.

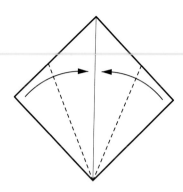

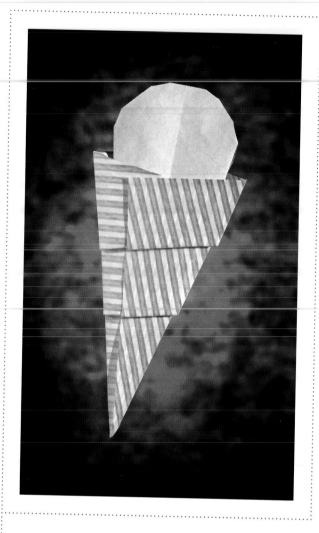

1. Precrease one diagonal. Valley-fold edges to centerline.

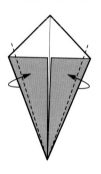

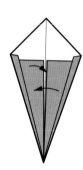

2. Narrow sides of cone slightly with valley-folds.

3. Pull out loose paper on each side, keeping the narrow flaps in place.

Ice Cream Cones

SINGLE-SCOOP CONES

Int.

A 6-inch (15-cm) square produces a cone that is 6 inches (15 cm) tall (not including scoop).

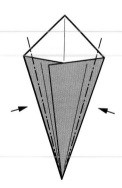

4. Reverse-fold along the creases formed in step 2.

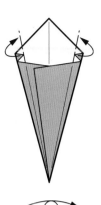

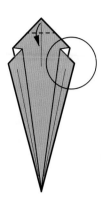

5. On each side, swing a narrow flap to the rear where it folds naturally. Turn over.

6. Valley-fold tip to begin rounding of ice cream. Circle indicates area of details in next step.

7.   7A.   7B.

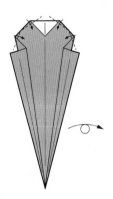

7. Valley-fold tiny flap to edge and swing loose paper down with another valley-fold.
7A. Turn loose paper inside out and tuck behind.
7B. Completed tuck. Repeat step 7 on other side.

8. Round top and sides of ice cream with valley-folds. Turn over.

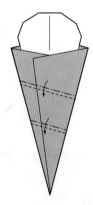

9. Optional: Form two tiny pleats to suggest the spiral shape of the cone. Each crease is perpendicular to the right-hand edge.

Completed Single-Scoop Cone.

DOUBLE-SCOOP CONE

An 8 ¹/₂-inch (21- to 22-cm) square produces a cone that is 6 inches (15 cm)
tall (not including scoops) to match the size of the single-scoop cone.

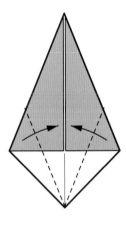

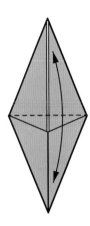

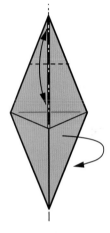

1. Begin with one diagonal
precreased and two edges
folded to centerline, as in
step 1 of the single-scoop
cone. Valley-fold two
lower edges to centerline.

2. Valley-fold entire model in
half and unfold.

2A. Valley-fold tip to center
of crease formed in pre-
vious step and unfold.
Mountain-fold entire
model in half vertically.

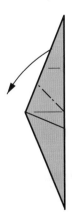

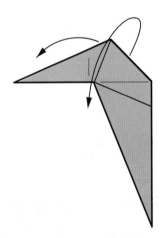

3. Inside reverse-fold so that edge of flap
becomes horizontal.

3A. Carefully open up top of model and turn
paper inside out along existing creases. No
new creases are formed. Flatten.

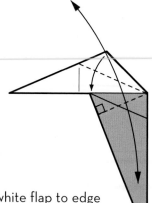

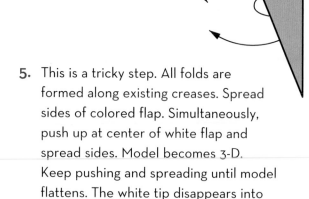

4. Valley-fold white flap to edge and repeat behind. Valley-fold colored portion perpendicular to left-hand edge and unfold.

5. This is a tricky step. All folds are formed along existing creases. Spread sides of colored flap. Simultaneously, push up at center of white flap and spread sides. Model becomes 3-D. Keep pushing and spreading until model flattens. The white tip disappears into the center of the colored flap.

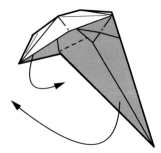

5A. 3-D drawing of the procedure from step 5 in progress.

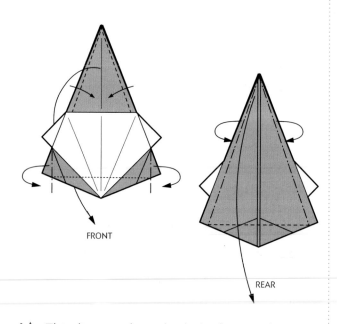

FRONT

REAR

6. Flatten. Valley-fold tiny flaps to adjacent colored edges and unfold.

6A. This diagram shows both the front and rear of the model. Reverse-fold tiny flaps along creases formed in previous step. Simultaneously, narrow the large colored flap at rear with valley-folds all the way to the tip and swing the colored tip down along a horizontal valley-fold (as seen on the rear). Assist the paper as it stretches. The model will eventually lie flat.

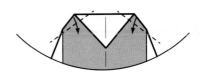

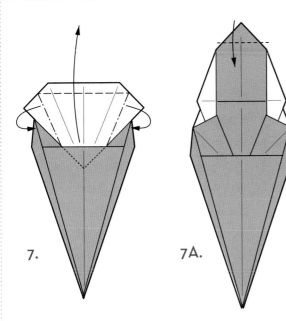

7.   **7A.**

7. Pull out the hidden white tip and swing the white flap upward, forming a new horizontal valley-fold. The sides of the white flap will begin to swing inward. When the sides have swung as far as they can (to where they are restrained by the colored paper) and the inner edges are vertical, flatten.

7A. Valley-fold tip to begin rounding of upper scoop.

7B. Add more tiny valley-folds to round tip. Turn model over.

8. Create tiny mountain-folds to begin rounding of lower scoop. Below, carefully pull out all layers of loose paper.

9. Add more tiny mountain-folds to complete rounding of upper scoop. Valley-fold sides of cone to align with edges on back, not edges on front.

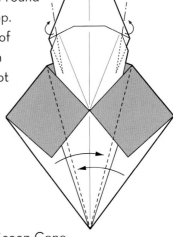

Completed Double-Scoop Cone. Reverse the front and back colors or use paper that is colored on both sides to form different flavors.

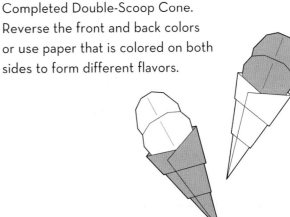

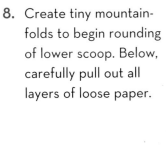

10. Optional: Form two tiny pleats to suggest the spiral shape of the cone. Each crease is perpendicular to the right-hand edge.

Chapter 3

....

FOR THE
ROMANTIC

VALENTINE ✳ Easy

A 10-inch (25-cm) square produces a valentine that is 7 inches (18 cm) square.

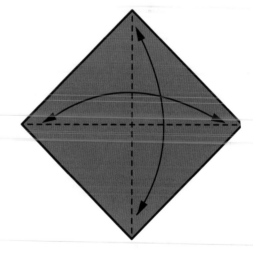

1. Valley-fold vertically and horizontally and unfold.

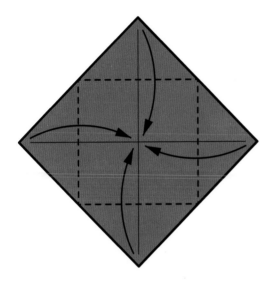

2. Valley-fold corners to center.

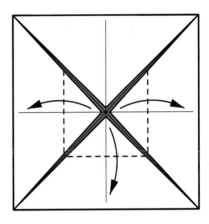

3. Valley-fold three corners back out, but not all the way to the edge.

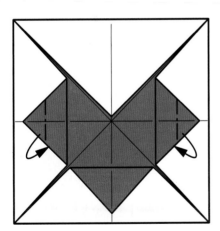

4. Mountain-fold two red corners behind. Mountain-fold entire model down the center-line to make the model stand or valley-fold to make a card with the valentine hidden.

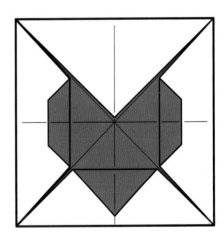

Completed Valentine.

PICTURE FRAME

*️⃣ Easy

A 10-inch (25-cm) square produces a picture frame with a 3 ½-inch (9-cm) square window.

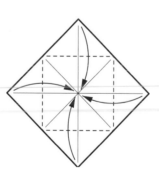

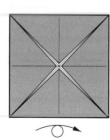

1. Precrease diagonals. Valley-fold corners to center.
1A. Turn over.

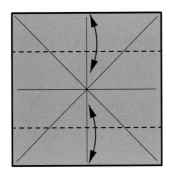

2. Valley-fold top and bottom edges to the horizontal centerline. Unfold.

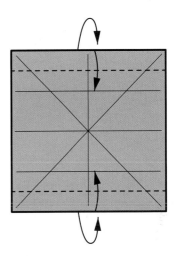

3. Valley-fold to the creases formed in the previous step and swing loose paper from back to front.

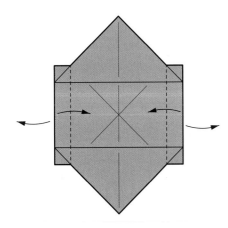

4. Repeat step 3 on left- and right-hand edges.

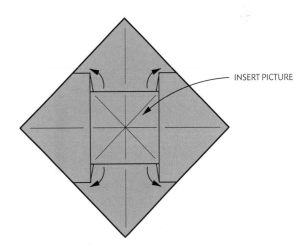

INSERT PICTURE

5. Pull out loose paper and flatten. Insert picture into the pocket.

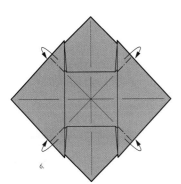

6. Reverse-fold four triangles behind to lock picture into place.

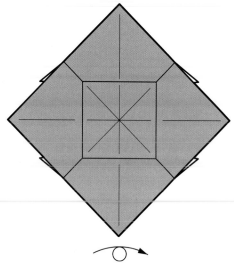

6A. Turn over.

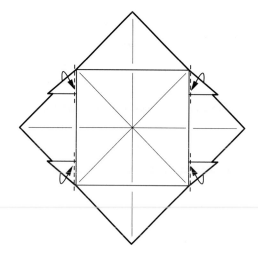

7. Valley-fold triangles into pockets. Turn over. To produce a fancier frame, complete step 7 and skip to step 9.

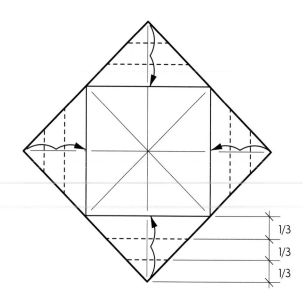

8. Roll each corner over and over.

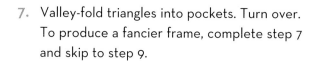

8A. Valley-fold four flaps into pockets to lock picture frame. Turn over.

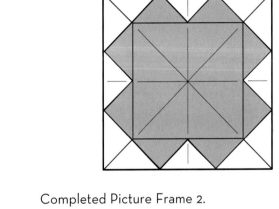

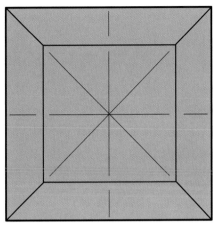

9. Turn over.

Completed Picture Frame 1.

Completed Picture Frame 2.

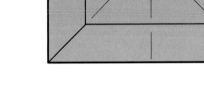

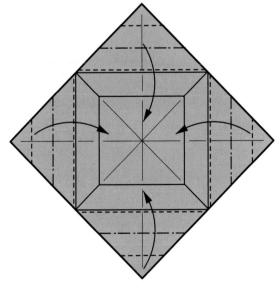

10. Alternate valley- and mountain-folds in an accordion fashion.

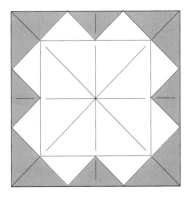

To produce a picture frame with the opposite coloration, begin with the colored side up.

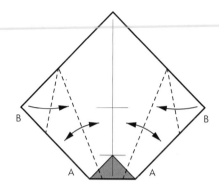

2A. Valley-fold lower edges to centerline and unfold.

2B. Valley-fold upper edges to crease formed in A. Then refold creases formed in A.

HIGH-HEELED SHOE

Adv.

A 10-inch (25-cm) square produces a shoe that is 6 1/4 inches (16 cm) long.

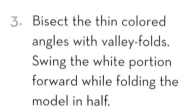

3. Bisect the thin colored angles with valley-folds. Swing the white portion forward while folding the model in half.

1. Precrease one diagonal. Lightly fold in half horizontally to produce a line at the 1/8 point. Valley-fold bottom tip upward at that line.

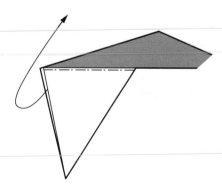

4. Reverse-fold the white portion up through the center of the model at the colored edge.

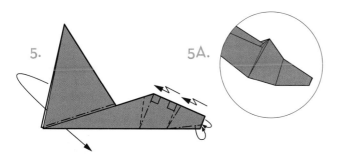

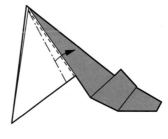

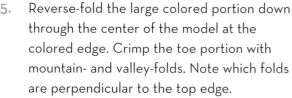

5. Reverse-fold the large colored portion down through the center of the model at the colored edge. Crimp the toe portion with mountain- and valley-folds. Note which folds are perpendicular to the top edge.

5A. When folding the crimp located closer to the rear of the shoe, a small vertical gusset will automatically form at the center of the model (see 3-D detail in 5A). Narrow the very tip of the shoe with mountain-folds on either side. Rotate the model so that the bottom of the toe is horizontal.

6. Crimp the white portion so that it bisects the long, narrow angle at the rear of the colored portion.

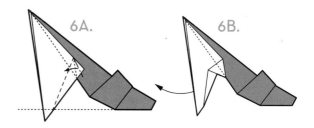

6A. Narrow the right side of the white portion with a valley-fold, stretching the upper right corner of the paper to form a small triangle. Note that the valley-fold does not go all the way to the bottom tip, but stops on the horizontal line formed by the bottom of the toe.

6B. Open out the white portion and refold symmetrically, turning creases inside out as necessary. No new creases are formed.

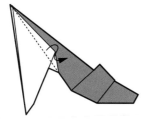

7. Tuck top of white portion under one layer of colored paper on each side.

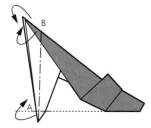

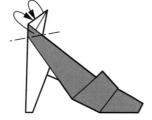

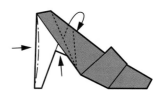

8A. Reverse-fold tip of heel up and inward.

8B. Mountain-fold sides of heel inward as far as they will go. Press firmly.

9. Mountain-fold exposed end flaps symmetrically into central cavity.

10. In central cavity, double over all interior thicknesses with tweezers to lock. Gently round back of heel and sole to complete the High-Heeled Shoe.

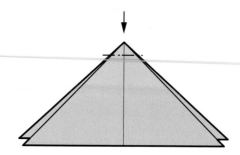

WEDDING RING ❖ Adv.

A 5-inch (13-cm) square produces a ring approximately ³/₄ inch (2 cm) in diameter.

2. Sink the upper pyramid at the crease formed in step 1. It will help to open out the paper slightly. The sunk portion of the paper forms a square before it becomes an inverted pyramid.

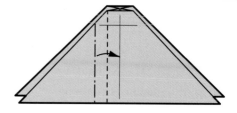

3. Valley-fold at edge of sink-crease and mountain-fold to meet vertical centerline.

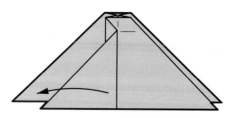

3A. Completed fold. Repeat on three other sides and unfold.

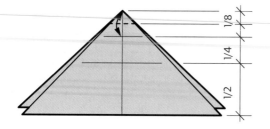

1. Precrease diagonals with mountain-folds and vertical and horizontal centerlines with valley-folds to form a pyramid. Lightly fold in half horizontally and crease firmly at the ¹/₈ point.

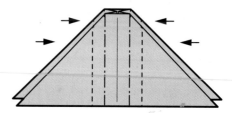

4. Reverse-fold all four flaps on existing creases to achieve image in next diagram.

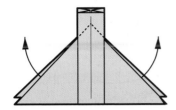

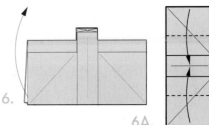

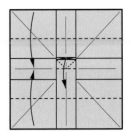

6.

6A.

5. The paper is vertical where the two flaps on each side come together. Swing the vertical paper upward along its centerline until it becomes horizontal. This is a kind of reverse-fold in that the crease at the centerline turns inside-out. No new creases are formed.

6. Swing up rear along horizontal centerline and flatten.

6A. Flatten inverted pyramid at center of paper to form a square. Valley-fold top and bottom edges to horizontal centerline and tuck under central square.

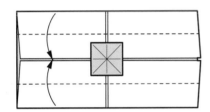

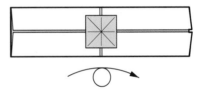

7. Valley-fold top and bottom edges to horizontal centerline and tuck under central square.

7A. Turn over.

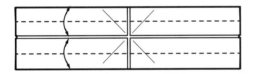

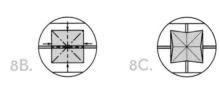

8A.

8B.   8C.

8. Valley-fold top and bottom edges to horizontal centerline. Crease firmly through many thicknesses and unfold.

8A. Valley-fold left edge and mountain-fold right edge to form flaps of equal size. Blow into hole at X to inflate jewel and see next step.

8B. Gently push insides of jewel to make 3-D.

8C. Completed jewel. Protect from flattening during remaining steps.

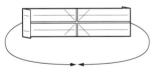

9. Roll band into a circle and interlock ends.

9A. Ends interlocked.

10. Carefully roll in top and bottom of band along creases formed in step 8. Band becomes thick but will hold together

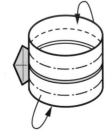

Completed Wedding Ring.

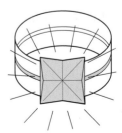

BUTTERFLY ◆ Adv.

A 10-inch (25-cm) square produces a duck that is
9 1/4 inches (24 cm) long from beak to tail.

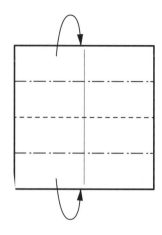

1. Pre-crease vertical centerline. Mountain- and valley-fold at quarter-points to form an accordion shape.

2. Valley-fold two front layers together from lower corners through upper middle.

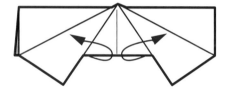

3. Pull out trapped paper and flatten.

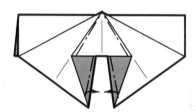

4. Swivel colored flaps slightly toward center and form new mountain-folds. Mountain-folds on white triangle will form automatically.

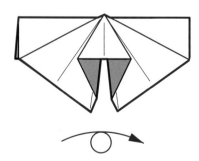

4A. Turn over.

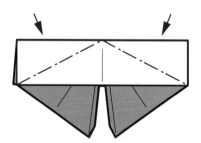

5. Reverse-fold through two front layers from lower corners through upper middle.

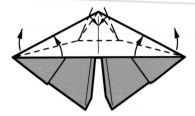

6. This is a complex maneuver. Narrow left and right corners of white triangle with valley-folds while simultaneously valley-folding bottom of white triangle upwards. Crimp the paper at the top of the white triangle toward the centerline to allow the paper to lie flat.

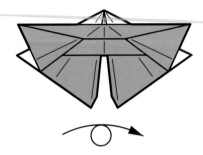

6A. Completed maneuver. Turn over.

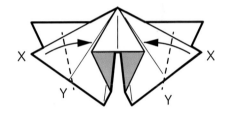

7. Valley-fold the white flaps on either side so that edge XY aligns with the sides of the central triangle. The paper behind will stretch. Flatten as shown in the next diagram.

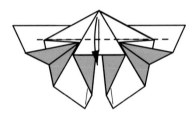

8. Valley-fold white flap downward at edge of flaps formed in previous step.

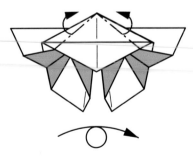

8A. Narrow sides of thick white paper with mountain-folds into pockets behind as far as pockets permit. Turn over.

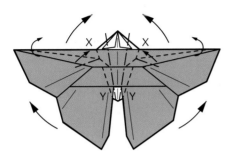

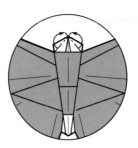

9. This is another difficult maneuver. First, valley-fold the full thickness of the paper on each side from X, where the top white paper meets colored paper, to Y, where the white bottom white paper meets colored paper. Crease firmly. Then mountain-fold the full thickness of the paper so that the valley-folds just produced meet at the centerline. This will cause the wings to rotate and will form the body shown in the next step. After the body is formed, narrow the front edges of the wings to a point not fully at the corner. See final diagram to see result.

9A. Narrow white triangle at top with mountain-folds. Tweezers will help with this and the following steps.

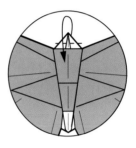

9B. Valley-fold white triangle downward so that its tip projects into the colored region.

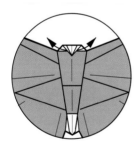

9C. Pull out hidden paper at either side of white triangl to form head.

Completed Butterfly. Optionally, valley-fold tips of wings to form patches of white or use paper colored on two sides to form patches of color.

Chapter 4

....

WILD KINGDOM

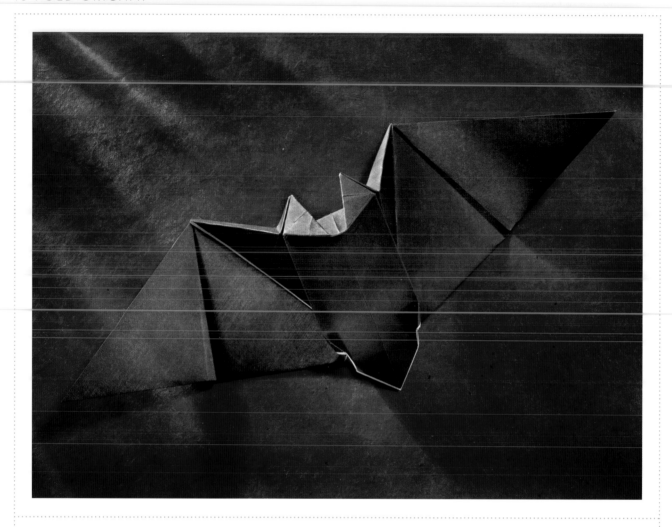

BAT

 Easy

A 10-inch (25-cm) square produces a bat with an 11-inch (28-cm) wingspan.

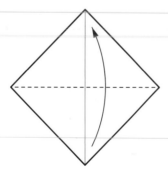

1. Precrease one diagonal. Valley-fold other diagonal.

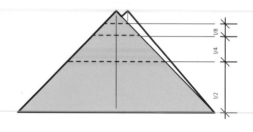

2. Lightly fold in half repeatedly to produce a line at the ⅛ point.

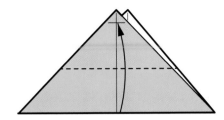

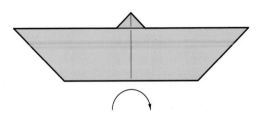

3. Firmly valley-fold bottom edge to the ⅛ line.

4. Rotate.

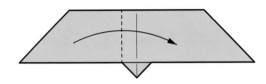

5. Valley-fold where edges meet.

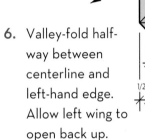

6. Valley-fold half-way between centerline and left-hand edge. Allow left wing to open back up.

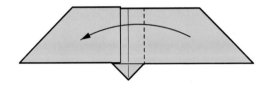

7. Repeat steps 5 and 6 on right-hand side.

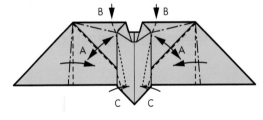

8. Turn over.

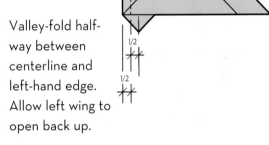

9A. Vertical valley-folds—crease and unfold.
9B. Grasp horizontal edge of paper with one finger, pull forward, and flatten to form face and ears.

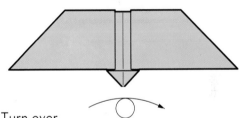

10A. Crimp wings with valley- and mountain-folds.
10B. Press at top of wings to shape ears.
10C. Form legs with tiny valley-folds.

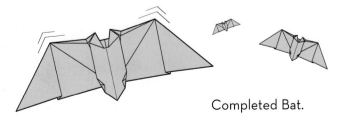

Completed Bat.

PENGUIN Int.

A 10-inch (25-cm) square produces a penguin that is 6 inches (15 cm) tall.

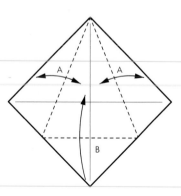

1. Precrease diagonals with valley-folds.
1A. Valley-fold edges to centerline and unfold.
1B. Valley-fold bottom tip where previous creases meet edge.

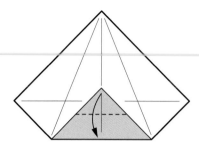

2. Valley-fold tip of colored triangle to bottom.

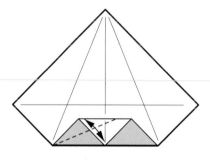

2A. Narrow colored angle in half with a valley-fold. Note that the fold passes the centerline. Unfold and repeat on right side.

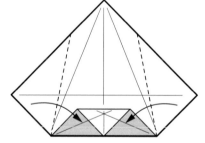

3. Valley-fold the two sides of the paper so that the lower edges meet the angled creases formed in the previous step.

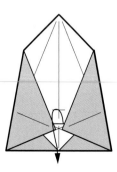

4. Swing the paper obscured in the previous step out and down.

5. Pinch on the existing crease between points X and Y. Valley-fold the white layer from Y to Z. The tiny valley-folds on the colored paper will form automatically.

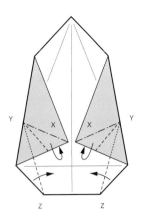

6. Valley-fold upward on existing crease.

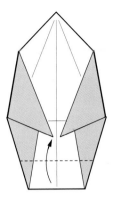

7. Valley-fold from point to point.

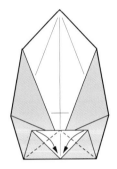

8. Mountain-fold the entire model in half.

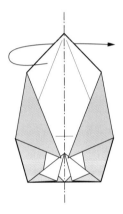

9. **Bottom:** Reverse-fold the central flap toward the rear of the penguin to separate the feet.
Top: Reverse-fold white flap through the point where white and black paper meet.

9A. Reverse-fold the same flap back toward the front of the penguin. This crease aligns with the edge where white and black paper meet.

9B. Valley-fold front and back to narrow head.

9C. Swivel the head and beak downward with tiny, hidden crimp folds.

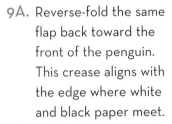

9.

9A.

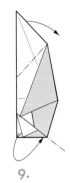

9B.

9C.

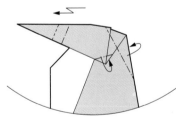

10. Two reverse-folds form the beak. Round back and bottom of head with mountain-folds on each side.

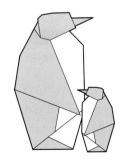

Completed Penguin.

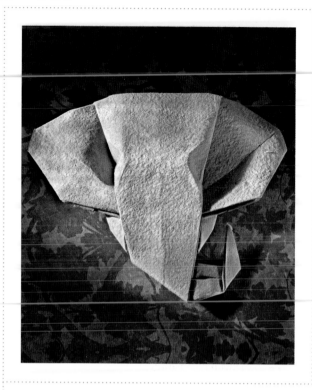

ELEPHANT HEAD ◆ Int.

A 10-inch (25-cm) square produces an elephant head that is 8 ¹⁄₄ (21 cm) inches from ear to ear.

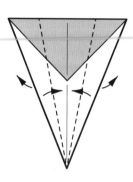

2. Valley-fold sides to centerline without creasing back flaps. Swing back flaps out to side.

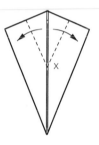 

3. Valley-fold from upper edges to hidden tip of colored paper, marked X. At upper end of valley-folds, paper stretches as far as it will go. Note that the corners of the paper that swing out do not fall directly on the outer corners of the white flaps (see next diagram).

4. Swivel the trapped paper outward. Mountain-folds will appear automatically. Flatten.

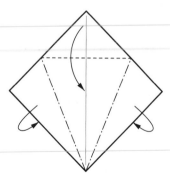

1. Precrease one diagonal. Mountain-fold sides behind to meet at centerline and valley-fold top downward.

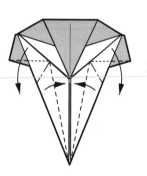

5. Narrow trunk with valley-folds. The upper portion of the paper on each side will swing down automatically.

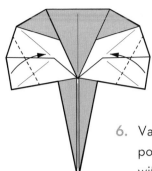

7.   7A.   7B.

6. Valley-fold so that outer portion of ear flaps aligns with interior crease.

7. Detail of right ear shown from rear. Mountain-fold a tiny flap so that WX is parallel to YZ.

7C.

7A. Valley-fold flap to edge.
7B. Valley-fold flap to edge.
7C. Swivel top flap and tuck into pocket underneath.

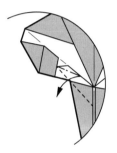

8. Valley-fold in order to expose white flap (tusk) adjacent to trunk on the other side of the model (see step 10). In order for the tusk to lie flat, the upper portion of the tusk will need to be stretched, squashed, and flattened into a tiny triangle. See next step.

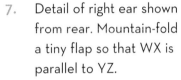

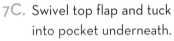

9. Stretched and flattened tiny triangle. The inner edge of the tusk is shown with a dotted line. Repeat steps 7 through 9 on the opposite side and turn model over.

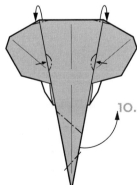

10. Round top of head with tiny mountain-folds. Round sides of head with mountain-folds to make head 3-D and to form eyes. Mountain-fold trunk twice to curve it upwards.

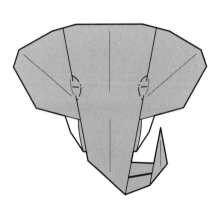

Completed Elephant Head.

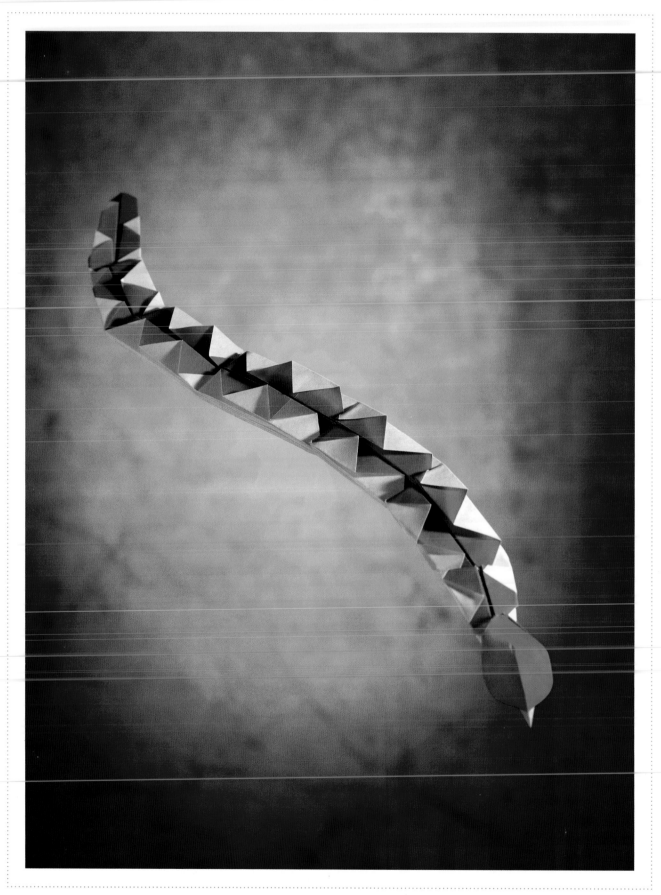

SNAKE

A 10-inch (25-cm) square produces a snake that is 11 inches (28 cm) long.

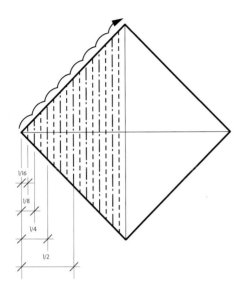

1. Precrease the diagonals. Divide the left-hand side vertically into sixteenths and form alternating valley- and mountain-folds in an accordion fashion.

2. Turn over.

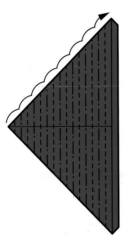

3. Divide the left-hand side vertically into sixteenths and accordion-fold as in step 1.

4. Mountain-fold the hidden colored layer and swing the upper, triangulated layer underneath. Do not actually crease the triangulated layer. (This will produce a colored snake with a white stripe and head as shown in the remaining diagrams. To produce a white snake with a colored stripe and head, turn model over before executing this step.)

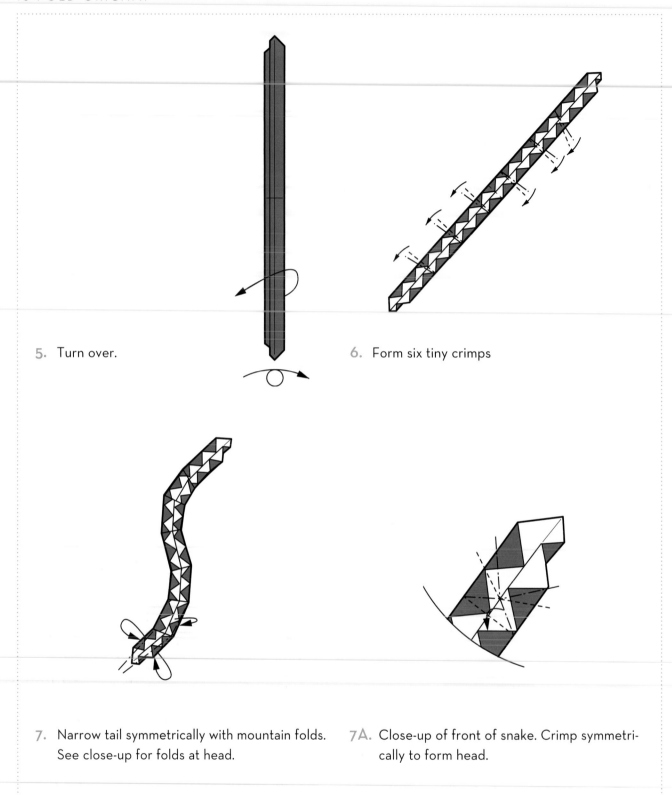

5. Turn over.

6. Form six tiny crimps

7. Narrow tail symmetrically with mountain folds. See close-up for folds at head.

7A. Close-up of front of snake. Crimp symmetrically to form head.

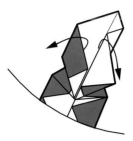

8. Carefully lift flaps at either side of head and turn inside out.

9. Mountain-fold head down the centerline and crimp front of head to form tongue. The head becomes 3-D.

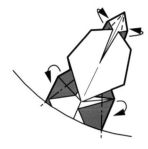

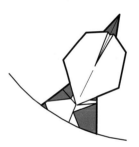

9A. Narrow tongue with valley-folds. Narrow body with mountain-folds just behind head.

10. Finished head.

Finished Snake, ready to slither.

Snail on an Ivy Leaf

IVY LEAF

A 10-inch (25-cm) square produces a leaf that is 11 inches (28 cm) from stem to tip.

1. Pre-crease the diagonals. Divide the left-hand side vertically into sixteenths and form alternating valley- and mountain-folds in an accordion fashion.

1/2   1/2

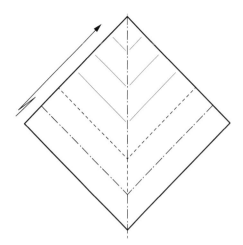

1A. Finished accordion-fold. Unfold.

2. Reverse-fold along two pairs of existing creases, as designated.

3. At the end of step 2, the leaf is symmetrical. Swing the rear portion (half of the leaf) behind the model so that the leaf becomes flat. No new creases are formed in this step.

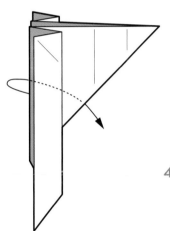

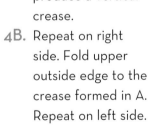

A   B

4A. Lightly valley-fold corner to center to produce a vertical crease.

4B. Repeat on right side. Fold upper outside edge to the crease formed in A. Repeat on left side.

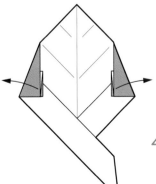

4C. Unfold.

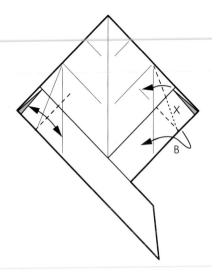
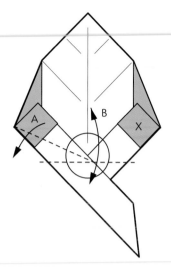

5A. Note where existing angled crease meets edge. Firmly valley-fold from that point parallel to the edge where thickness occurs. Repeat on right side.

5B. This is a difficult step requiring that the paper open out in three dimensions before flattening. Pinch the uppermost layer at X. Pull out to release trapped paper. Simultaneously valley-fold on existing visible and hidden creases, swinging colored paper over to the left. Then collapse paper to position shown in step 6. Repeat on left side.

6A. Swing down on angled valley-fold where the fold forms naturally. The colored portion of the paper will flatten smoothly. Note that the valley-fold goes past the centerline of the model.

6B. Valley-fold stem upwards where the valley-fold from A meets the edge of the stem. Unfold stem back down.

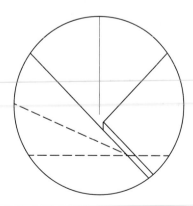

6C. Close-up of top of stem.

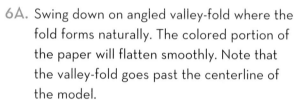

7. Grasp loose colored paper and swing out from underneath. This will free up loose white paper on the stem. Crimp at stem so paper lies flat.

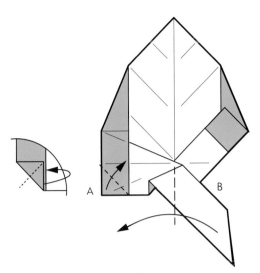

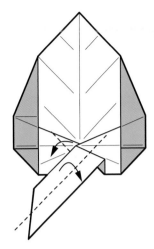

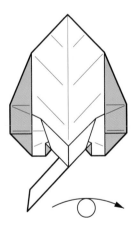

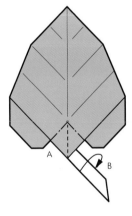

8A. Valley-fold tiny triangle.
Optional: With tweezers, fold in half and tuck under to lock.

8B. Swing stem to left at centerline, then repeat steps 6 through 8 on right side.

9A. Narrow stem in half with a valley-fold. White paper at top of stem will automatically spread open. Flatten.

9B. Spreading and flattening completed. Turn over.

10A. Press in at top of stem to make leaf 3-D.

10B. Optional: For a colored stem, grasp outer-most single ply of white paper. Carefully spread stem, turn paper inside out, and flatten.

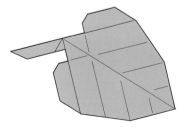

Completed Ivy Leaf.

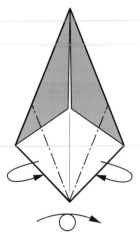

SNAIL

A 10-inch (25-cm) square produces a snail that is 4 $^3/_4$ inches (12 cm) long

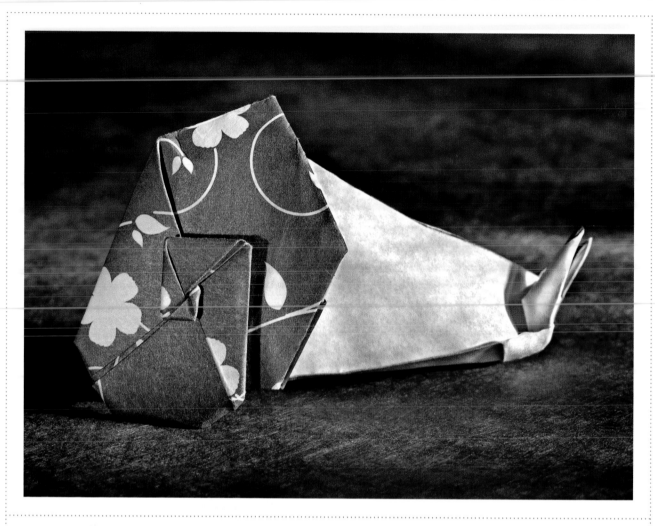

1. Pre-crease one diagonal and fold two edges to center-line to produce the kite shape shown. Mountain-fold two edges underneath as far as they will go.

2. Mountain-fold two flaps behind to meet centerline. Turn over.

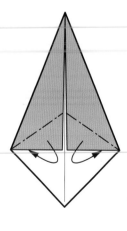

3. Valley-fold white tip to where white and colored paper meet. Unfold.

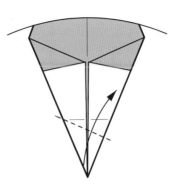

3A. Form a valley-fold where horizontal crease formed in previous step meets left-hand edge. Folded paper falls exactly upon edge.

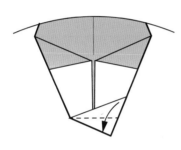

3B. Valley-fold white triangle edge to edge, bisecting left-hand angle. Unfold. Repeat this and the previous step on the opposite side.

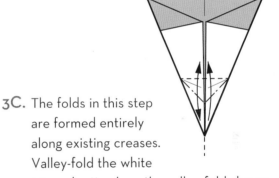

3C. The folds in this step are formed entirely along existing creases. Valley-fold the white triangular tip along the valley-fold shown and simultaneously spread the sides. If you flatten the sides forming the mountain-folds shown (only on the top, white layer), the paper will lay flat. Swing the tip to the left. See next diagram.

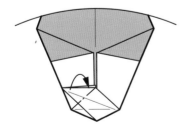

4. Reverse-fold tip of white paper along existing crease.

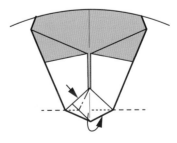

5. Narrow central flap with a reverse-fold and swing entire assembly underneath along existing horizontal crease.

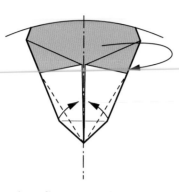

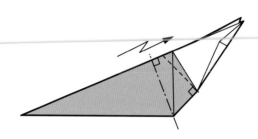

6. Narrow white flaps on either side with valley-folds, then mountain-fold entire model in half and orient as shown in next step.

7. Mountain-fold perpendicular to upper edge and valley-fold perpendicular to lower edge, then reverse-fold symmetrically.

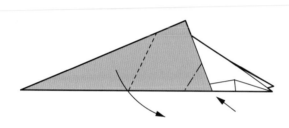

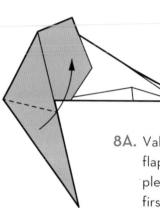

8. Reverse-fold triangle at right side, front and back. Optional: twist and flatten paper inside with tweezers to lock front portion of shell. Valley-fold rear of shell forward to begin spiral. To locate the fold-line, see next diagram.

8A. Valley-fold triangular flap six times to complete spiral. After the first valley-fold, each succeeding fold causes the triangular flap to align with an existing edge of the shell.

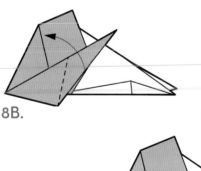

8B.

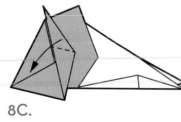

8C.

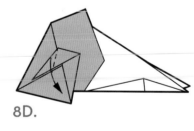

8D.

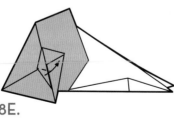

8E.

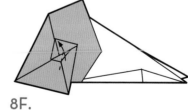

8F.

9. Details of head. Valley-fold front antenna as far to the left as it will go.

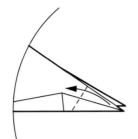

9A. Divide each angle of the little triangle with valley-folds and crimp upwards.

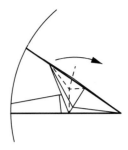

9B. Pull out loose paper and swing to front.

9C. Tuck loose paper into pocket within antenna. Repeat previous steps on rear antenna. Pull out loose horizontal paper to form mantle around snail's "foot."

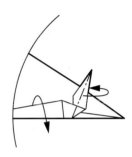

10. Round and spread at W to make shell 3-D. Tuck tiny tip of spiral underneath adjacent flap at X to lock. Reverse-fold rear of shell at Y. Optional: twist and flatten paper inside with tweezers to lock rear of shell. Mountain-fold lower tip of shell at Z into back flap to keep shell from springing outward. Press in and curve white paper at top to form head.

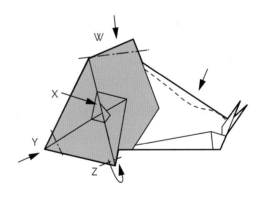

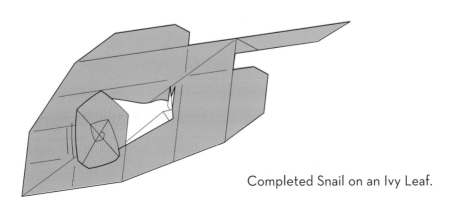

Completed Snail on an Ivy Leaf.

Chapter 5

....

JUST FOR FUN

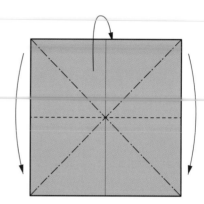

1. Pre-crease vertical centerline. Simultaneously mountain-fold diagonals and valley-fold horizontal centerline to achieve image in step 2.

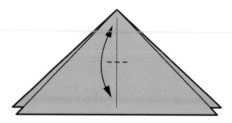

2. Valley-fold tip lightly to bottom and crease at centerline. Unfold.

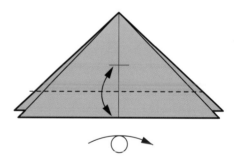

3. Valley-fold edge firmly to mark and unfold.

ROCKET
SHIP

A 10-inch (25-cm) square produces a rocket ship that is 11 inches (28 cm) long.

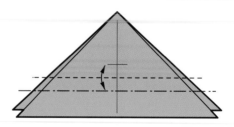

4. Valley-fold new crease firmly to mark and unfold. Open up entire square.

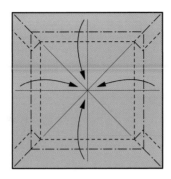

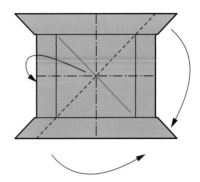

5. Mountain- and valley-fold on concentric squares formed in the last two steps. As the edges are pushed toward the center, new creases will automatically form at the corners as shown. Flatten.

6. Mountain- and valley-fold on existing center-lines to collapse paper.

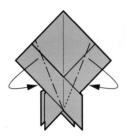

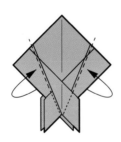

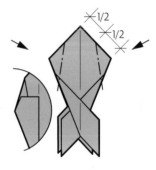

7. Mountain-fold the two front flaps so that edges meet the centerline.

8. Valley-fold the two rear flaps in the same fashion.

9. Reverse-fold the edges of the two front flaps to create tiny pockets. Inset: Interior view of pocket.

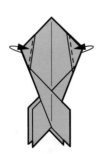

10. Valley-fold the edges of the two rear flaps into the tiny pockets in the front flaps to lock. Spread out the four fins at base.

Completed Rocket Ship.

SPINNER

A 10-inch (25-cm) square produces a spinner that is 5 inches (13 cm) in diameter.

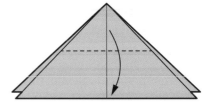

1. Begin with paper folded as in step 2 of the Rocket Ship. Valley-fold tip firmly to bottom.

2. Valley-fold left side of little triangle to meet top horizontal edge.

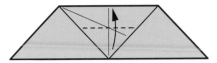

3. Valley-fold tip of little triangle up firmly where angled crease crosses centerline.

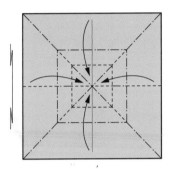

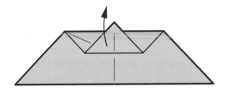

3A. Open up entire square.

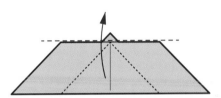

3B. Mountain and valley-fold on concentric squares formed in the earlier steps, collapsing the paper back into a shape similar to that in step 1. Specifically, the inner concentric square needs to consist of four valley-folds, and the outer one of four mountain-folds, as shown. You will need to turn some of the creases inside-out to achieve this configuration of folds. Once you do this, the little square at the center will stick out as a little pyramid, and the next square will be a portion of an upside-down pyramid. Flatten. Once the paper is flattened, the tiny tip of the central pyramid will stick out the top. This will be the tip that touches the table when you twirl the spinner. Throughout the remaining steps, be extremely careful not to crush this point.

4. Lift single-ply front flap and swing it upward, spreading and flattening the inner white flaps in the process. The triangular tip remains flat and unaffected by this move.

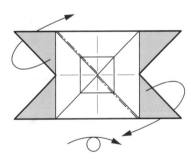

5. Grasp the upper left white flap and swivel it up and to the right. Grasp the lower right white flap and swivel it down and to the left. The triangular tip will no longer lie flat. Turn over. The next diagram shows these moves from the back.

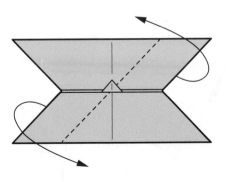

5A. View of step 5 from the back.

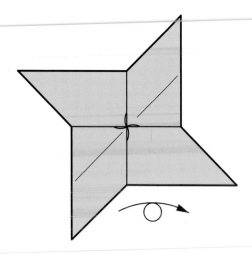

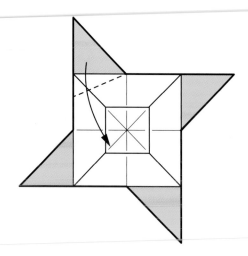

5B. Completed fold. The triangular tip is 3-D. Turn over.

6. Valley-fold one white flap to align with vertical centerline.

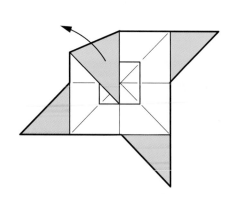

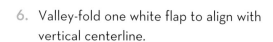

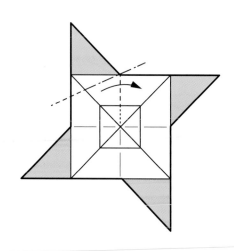

6A. Unfold flap.

7. Folding entirely on existing creases, swing the white flap to the right and flatten downward. Lift the paper in front of it slightly so that it has room to swing.

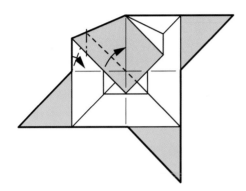

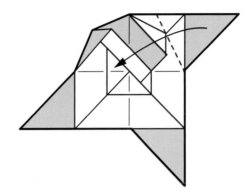

8. Valley-fold the colored paper directly over the main diagonal hidden beneath it. The colored paper will crimp automatically.

9. Repeat steps 6 through 8 on three other white flaps. Note that rotating the model a quarter-turn counterclockwise allows it to line up with position in step 6.

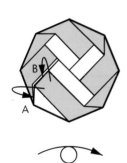

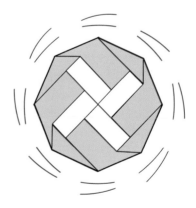

10. The fourth flap lies on top and needs to be tucked underneath.

10A. Tuck the white flap into the colored pocket beneath it.

10B. Tuck the colored-and-white flap under the adjoining white flap. The model is now fully symmetrical. Turn over to see reverse.

Completed Spinner. Place on a smooth surface, lightly grasp two opposite edges, and give it a whirl. Alternatively, toss it onto a smooth surface with a flick of the wrist, as if tossing a Frisbee.

GOLDEN EGG ◆ Int.

A 10-inch (25-cm) square produces an egg that is 7 inches (18 cm) long.

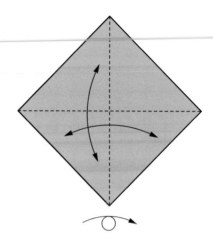

1. Valley-fold both diagonals. Turn over.

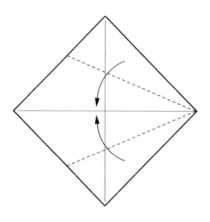

2. Valley-fold two edges to centerline.

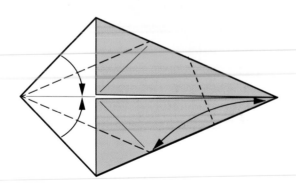

3. **Left side:** Valley-fold two edges to centerline. **Right side:** Valley-fold tip to where existing crease meets edge, and unfold.

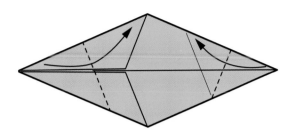

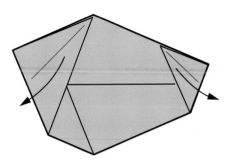

4. **Left side:** Valley-fold tip to point.
   Right side: Valley-fold tip to where crease meets edge.

5. Unfold two flaps.

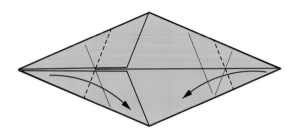

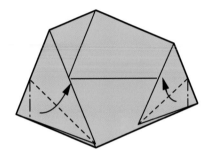

6. Valley-fold so each flap edge lands on the outer edge of the paper (the fold line is perpendicular to the edge). Locate fold lines where the creases formed in step 4 cross the centerline.

7. Narrow flaps with valley-folds so that hidden paper folds along existing creases. Mountain-folds form automatically. The mountain-folds that form automatically fall on existing creases, so if your folds are crisp, it should be clear where to flatten the paper.

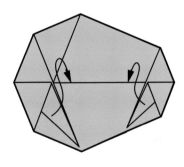

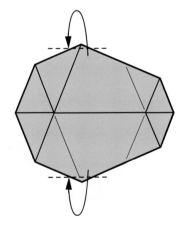

8. Lift single-ply paper at centerline and carefully tuck narrow flaps beneath. No new creases are formed.

9. Round top and bottom of egg and other corners as desired with tiny valley-folds or sink-folds. Turn over to complete the Golden Egg.

GOOSE

A 10-inch (25-cm) square produces a goose that is 6 ½ inches (16 to 17 cm) long. To produce a goose that will lay a golden egg, use a square for the goose that is approximately five times as long as the square for the egg.

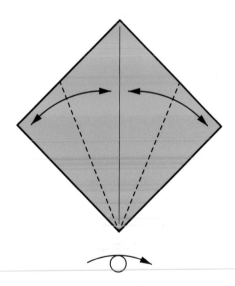

1. Precrease one diagonal. Valley-fold edges to centerline and unfold. Turn over.

2. Valley-fold where existing mountain-fold meets edge and crimp.

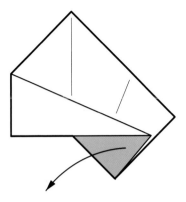

2A. Unfold and repeat on other side.

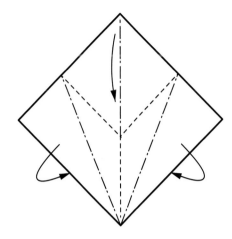

3. Mountain- and valley-fold on existing creases (as shown) to collapse model; be careful not to fold where creases are not shown. The paper comes together at the two long mountain-folds. The uppermost corner swings toward you. Once the paper is flat, the uppermost corner appears in step 4 as the point at the top, and the lowermost corner appears in step 4 as the point to the far left.

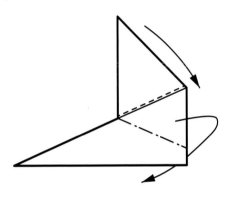

4. Valley-fold top flap where it meets the folded edge and unfold. Then swing top flap symmetrically through the center of the model, creating a new mountain-fold on either side. The upper flap should come to rest when its top edge lies horizontally, as shown in the next diagram.

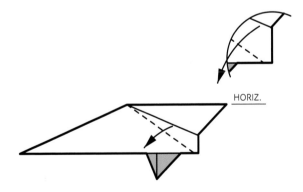

4A. Valley-fold small flap on either side. The crease does not go all the way to the corner, as shown in the detail.

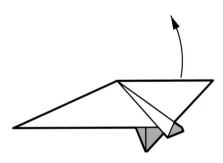

4B. Pull the top flap all the way out, keeping the small flap folded in the previous step in the same position.

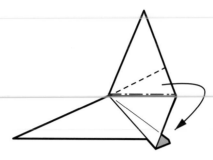

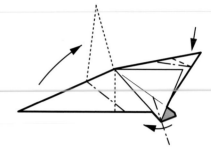

5. Crimp the top flap symmetrically. Mountain-fold at the existing crease line. Valley-fold so that the upper flap comes to rest approximately in the position shown in the next diagram.

6. Crimp tail symmetrically. Swing foot to front of model on each side with a tiny mountain-fold. In a difficult procedure, reverse-fold neck. The creases extend past the bottom of the flap (shown where dotted line meets the horizontal bottom edge of the body). Poke a finger into the cavity inside neck and spread interior layers at the bottom just enough to reverse-fold neck as shown. The paper will flatten.

7. Mountain-fold tiny white flaps of paper at feet upward to produce colored feet. Narrow neck with valley-folds on either side and tuck loose paper into body with tiny mountain-folds. Rotate body slightly so that it stands on base of feet. Body completed.

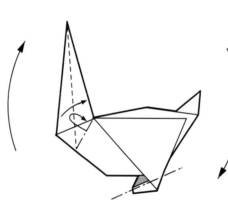

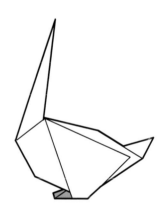

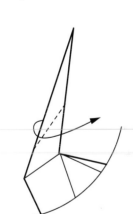

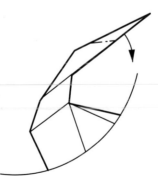

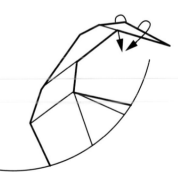

8. Valley-fold neck.

8A. Inside reverse-fold neck.

8B. Very carefully, spread sides of paper and turn inside out.

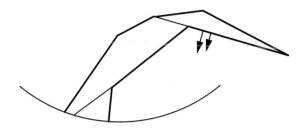 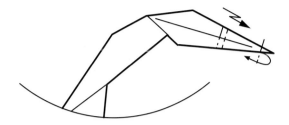

8C. Pull out trapped paper to enlarge head.

9. Reverse-fold head to form beak and tuck in tip.

10. Optional: If there is sufficient loose paper, open up beak, turn loose paper inside-out, and close up to produce a colored beak. Completed head shown with white and colored beak options.

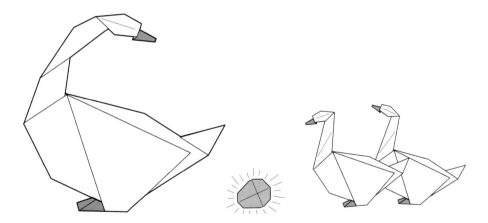

Completed Goose. Insert Golden Egg into hollow at back of tail.
When goose waddles, egg will fall out.

HATCHING
CHICK ◆ Adv.

A 10-inch (25-cm) square produces a chick
hatching from a 5-inch (13 cm) long egg.

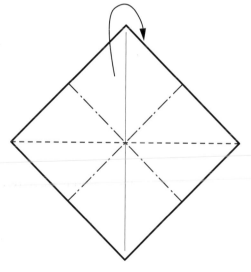

1. Precrease centerlines with mountain- and
   valley-folds and collapse as shown in next
   diagram.

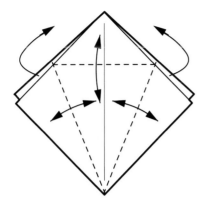

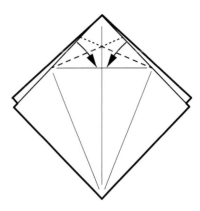

2. Valley-fold edges front and back to the vertical centerline and unfold. Valley-fold top triangle down and unfold.

2A. Valley-fold upper edges to horizontal crease formed in previous step. Crease firmly only to vertical centerline.

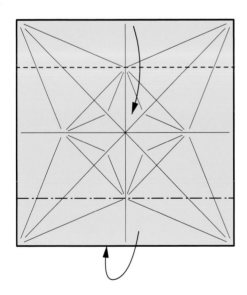

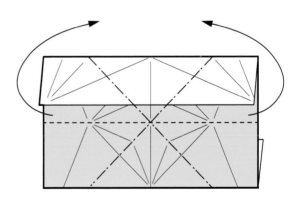

3. Unfold to original square with the colored side up. Valley-fold upper edge and mountain-fold lower edge at intersections as shown.

3A. Mountain- and valley-fold and collapse paper upward (collapsing sides underneath) to achieve the image in step 4. This procedure is similar to step 1. All folds fall on existing creases on one layer of the paper and the very center of the paper (where all the creases intersect) remains in the same position.

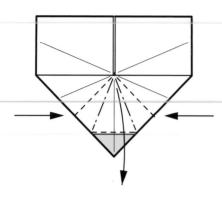

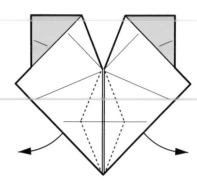

4. This is a tricky procedure. Grasp front white flap at middle of top edge. Swing triangular portion down so that a horizontal valley-fold forms on the existing crease as shown. Gently push in at sides to collapse paper inward. The model becomes 3-D before it flattens. All folds fall on existing creases on one layer of the paper.

4A. Dotted lines show the hidden thick flaps just formed. Pull out loose white paper and flatten on existing creases.

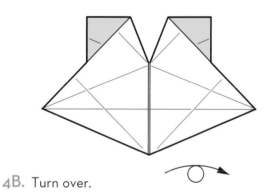

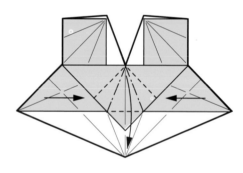

4B. Turn over.

5. Repeat previous sequence of folds on colored flap.

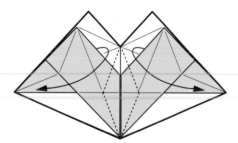

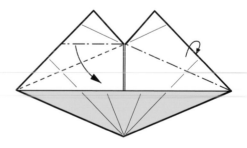

5A. Pull out loose colored paper.

5B. **Left side:** Swing large white flap down so that edge becomes vertical and creases align (see next diagram).
Right side: Reverse-fold large white flap.

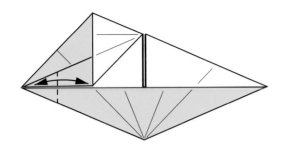 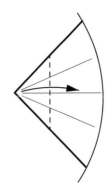 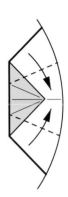

6. Valley-fold tip to where vertical edge of white flap meets the horizontal centerline, and unfold. Open up tip to reveal white side of paper. Details: Valley-fold on crease just formed. Close tip.

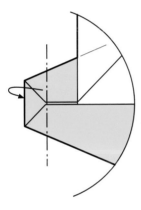

6A. Mountain-fold on existing crease.

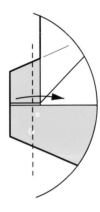

6B. Valley-fold so that left-hand edge of colored flap falls directly on colored edge behind it.

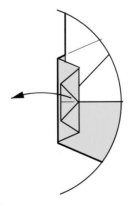

6C. Left-hand edges align (diagram shows a slight gap for clarity). Press firmly and unfold.

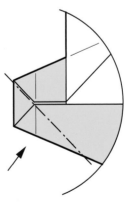

6D. Reverse-fold lower portion of tip along diagonal edge. It may help to valley-fold firmly first.

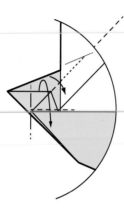

6E. Valley-fold colored flap at horizontal centerline while simultaneously valley-folding upper portion of tip. This valley-fold is a mirror image of the diagonal fold formed in the previous diagram.

6F. Pull out loose white paper and flatten on existing creases. No new creases are formed.

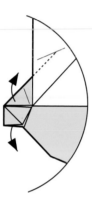

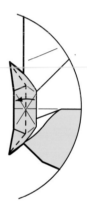

7A. 3-D drawing of collapse in progress.

7. This is a difficult step. Grasp triangular flaps on each side of centerline. Pull apart from each other, stretching the paper between them and forming a vertical mountain-fold. Gently collapse the paper along existing creases. Several new short creases are formed.

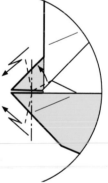

7B. Paper fully collapsed. Valley-fold edges to centerline along existing creases.

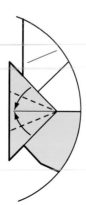

8. Carefully crimp upper and lower beaks with vertical mountain-folds and angled valley-folds. Tuck crimped portions into tiny pockets behind. Valley-fold a small triangle of paper (both thicknesses), stretching as far as possible, to form the eye.

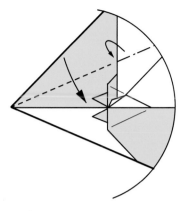

8A. Reverse-fold the large white and colored flap along existing creases.

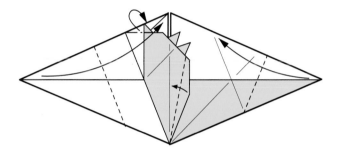

9A. **Top:** Reverse-fold tiny white and colored flap into pocket.
Middle: Valley-fold narrow colored flap to centerline.
Left and right: Form egg by folding steps 4 through 8 of the Golden Egg. On the right side, fold both layers together.

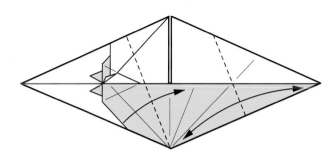

9. **Left side:** Valley-fold flap containing head up and to the right.
Right side: Valley-fold both thicknesses of paper from tip to tip and unfold.

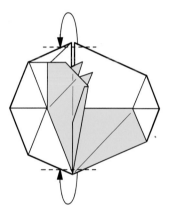

9B. Round top and bottom of egg and other corners as desired with tiny valley-folds or sink-folds. Turn over.

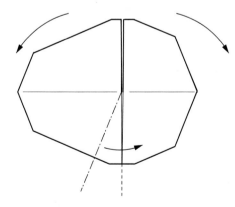

10. Crimp entire thickness of egg from center to bottom edge with a valley-fold along the vertical centerline and a mountain-fold perpendicular to the angled edge.

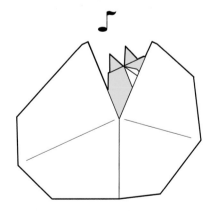

Open and close egg to reveal the completed Hatching Chick.

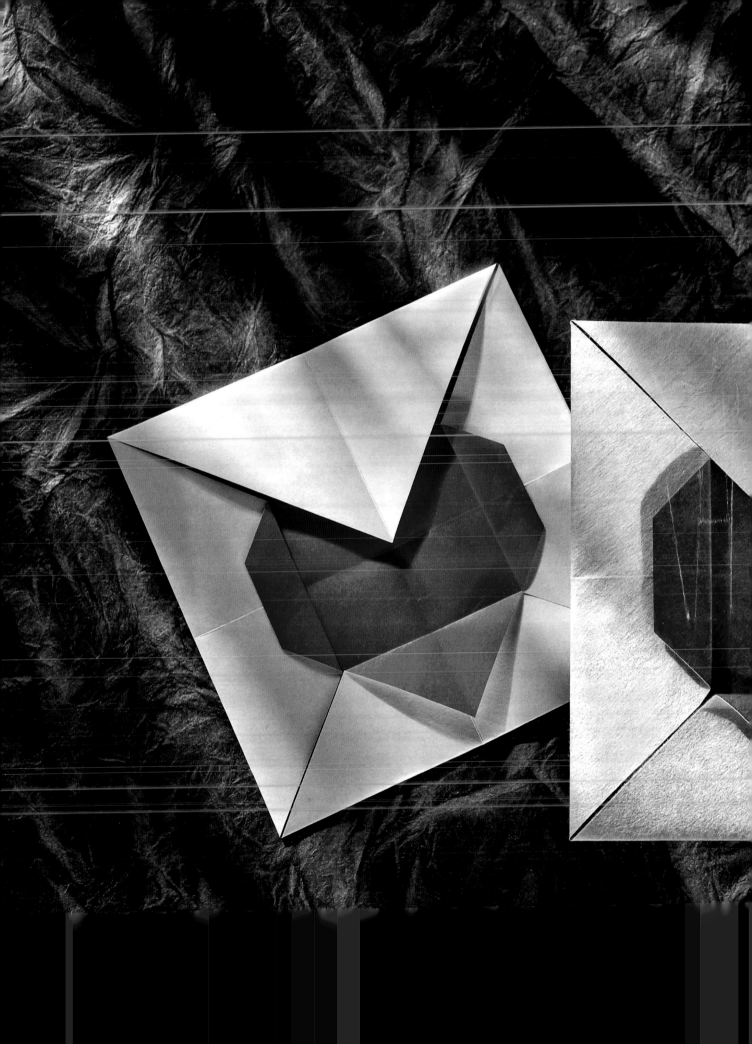

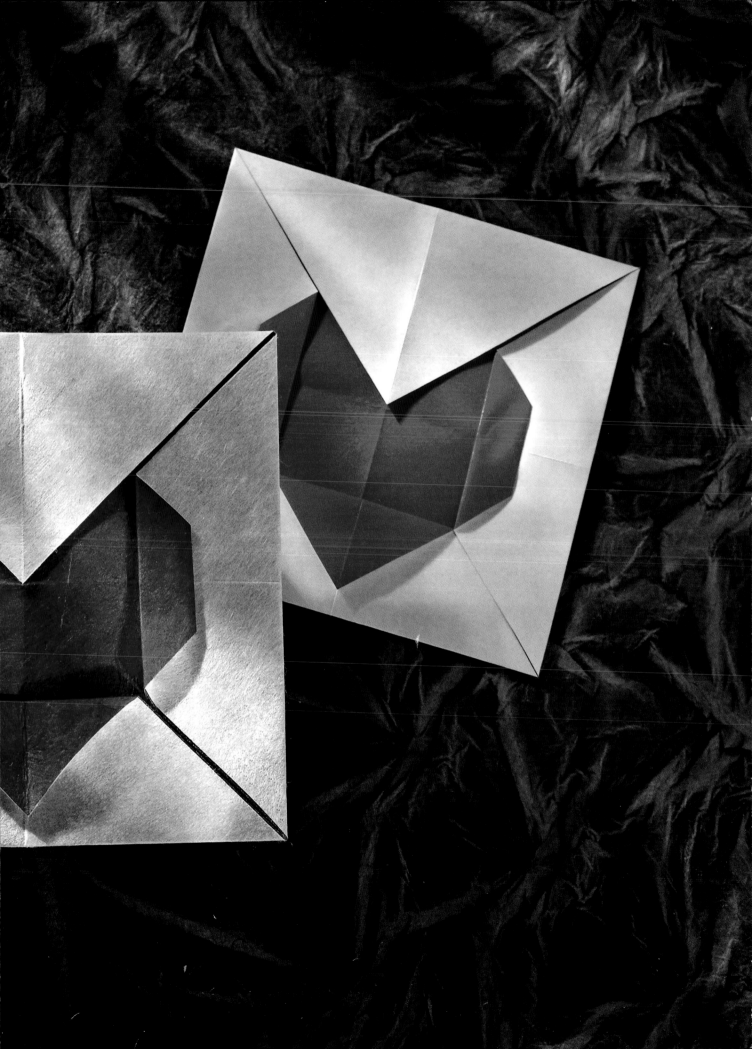

Acknowledgments

Thanks to my editor, Wendy Gardner, art director, Wendy Simard, assistant art director Seth Dolinsky, and their colleagues at Hollan Publishing for their hard work, keen judgment, and patience, and to Barbara Llewellyn for skillful drafting of the diagrams and abundant good humor. My parents and brother have encouraged my passion for origami since I was a child, and perhaps only they can appreciate what this art form has meant to me. Finally, I thank my wife, Cheryl, and our children, Hannah and Gabriel, for their unquestioning love and support.

About the Author

The origami designs of Peter Engel are known to paperfolding enthusiasts worldwide. The author of *Folding the Universe: Origami from Angelfish to Zen*, Engel has been creating original origami designs for over three decades. He has exhibited his origami artwork and sculpture at the Gettysburg College Art Gallery in Pennsylvania, the Asian Art Museum and the de Young Museum in San Francisco, the Carpenter Center for Visual Arts at Harvard University, the American Museum of Natural History in New York City, and Seian University of Art and Design in Otsu, Japan. The recipient of a Fulbright Fellowship and grants from the National Endowment for the Humanities, the Asian Cultural Council, and the Graham Foundation, Engel is a licensed architect in Berkeley, California with a practice specializing in schools, children's museums, ecological design, and international development. He and his wife Cheryl Perko have two children, Hannah and Gabriel.